W9-APD-268

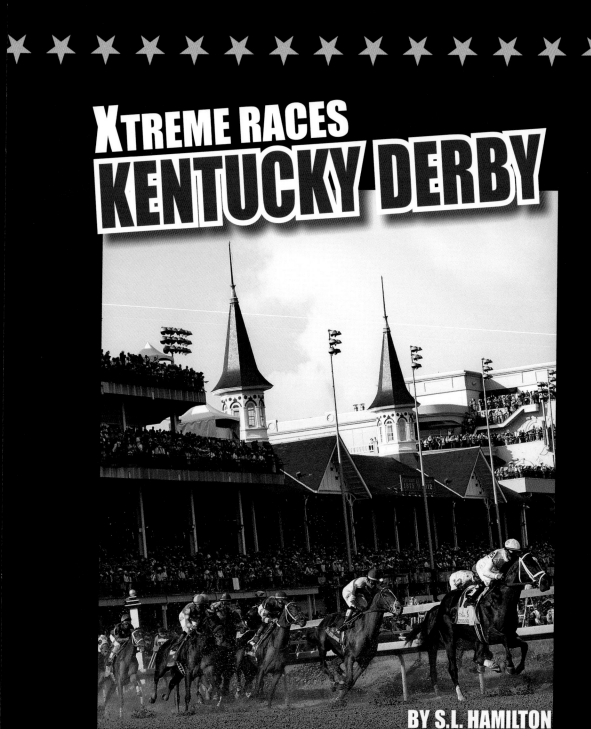

XTREME RACES
KENTUCKY DERBY

BY S.L. HAMILTON

Visit us at
www.abdopublishing.com

Published by ABDO Publishing Company, PO Box 398166, Minneapolis, MN 55439.
Copyright ©2013 by Abdo Consulting Group, Inc. International copyrights reserved in all
countries. No part of this book may be reproduced in any form without written permission
from the publisher. A&D Xtreme™ is a trademark and logo of ABDO Publishing Company.

Printed in the United States of America, North Mankato, Minnesota.
112012
012013

 PRINTED ON RECYCLED PAPER

Editor: John Hamilton
Graphic Design: Sue Hamilton
Cover Design: John Hamilton
Cover Photos: Getty
Interior Photos: AP-pgs 2-3, 8-9, 18-19, 21 (bottom), 22 (top, middle 2nd left, middle 2nd
right), 23 (bottom), 24 (bottom), 25 (bottom right), 26, 28, 29 & 32; Corbis-pgs 4-5, 18,
21 (top & middle), 22 (middle right, bottom middle, bottom right), 23 (top left & middle),
25 (top left & bottom left) & 30-31; Getty Images-pgs 10-17, 23 (top right), 25 (top right)
& 27; Library of Congress-pgs 6-7 & 24 (top right), National Museum of Racing and Hall of
Fame-pg 22 (Old Rosebud).

ABDO Booklinks
Web sites about Xtreme Races are featured on our Book Links pages. These links are
routinely monitored and updated to provide the most current information available.
Web site: www.abdopublishing.com

Cataloging-in-Publication Data

Hamilton, Sue L., 1959-
 Kentucky Derby / S.L. Hamilton.
  p. cm. -- (Xtreme races)
Includes index.
ISBN 978-1-61783-695-4
1. Kentucky Derby--History--Juvenile literature. 2. Kentucky Derby--Juvenile literature.
3. Horse racing--Kentucky--Juvenile literature. 4. Churchill Downs (Louisville, Ky. :
Racetrack--History--Juvenile literature. I. Title.
798.4006--dc23
                            2012945885

TABLE OF CONTENTS

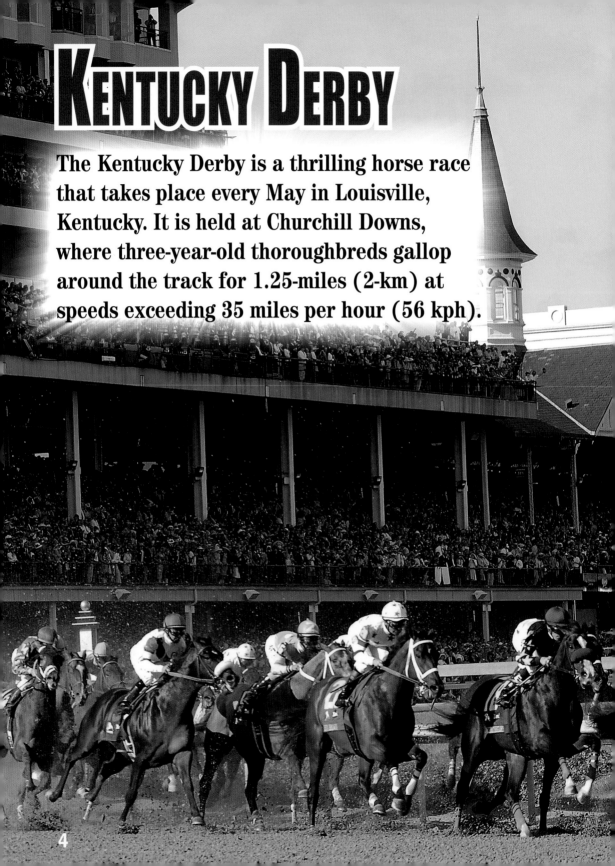

KENTUCKY DERBY

The Kentucky Derby is a thrilling horse race that takes place every May in Louisville, Kentucky. It is held at Churchill Downs, where three-year-old thoroughbreds gallop around the track for 1.25-miles (2-km) at speeds exceeding 35 miles per hour (56 kph).

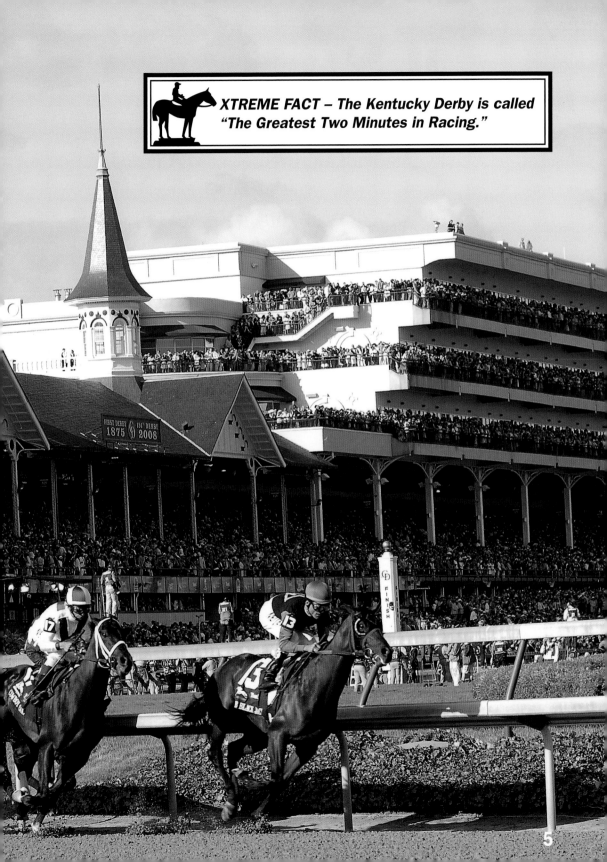

XTREME FACT – *The Kentucky Derby is called "The Greatest Two Minutes in Racing."*

HISTORY

American Meriwether Lewis Clark Jr. saw exciting horse races while traveling in Europe in 1872 and 1873. Clark went home to Kentucky and organized the Louisville Jockey Club. Members helped start a local racetrack.

XTREME FACT – The prize money for the first Kentucky Derby totaled $2,850–about $58,000 today.

Land for the racetrack came from Clark's uncles, John and Henry Churchill. Churchill Downs, as it came to be called, held its first Kentucky Derby in 1875. More than 10,000 fans watched jockey Oliver Lewis ride the thoroughbred Aristides for the win. The Kentucky Derby became known as "America's Race." It grew to be one of the most important horse races in the world.

Churchill Downs during the 1901 Kentucky Derby.

QUALIFYING

To qualify to run in the Kentucky Derby, horses compete in a series of races weeks before the Derby. The top finishers of these qualifying races earn a certain number of points.

The 20 thoroughbreds with the highest number of points earn their place in the Kentucky Derby. This is known as the "Road to the Kentucky Derby."

Horses race in the 2011 Blue Grass Stakes in Lexington, Kentucky. This is one of the races that helps thoroughbreds qualify for the Kentucky Derby.

XTREME FACT – If horses qualify with the same number of points, then the horse that wins the most money gets into the Derby.

THE START

The Kentucky Derby begins when the horses go to the starting gate. Each horse and jockey are led to a steel-gated stall by a start crew member. It's a tense time as the horse, jockey, and crew member wait for the starting bell.

One person, known as the starter at Churchill Downs, has the job of pushing the button that electronically opens all the gates at once. When the horses are settled and the riders ready, the button is pushed. Bells ring out and the announcer yells, "They're off!"

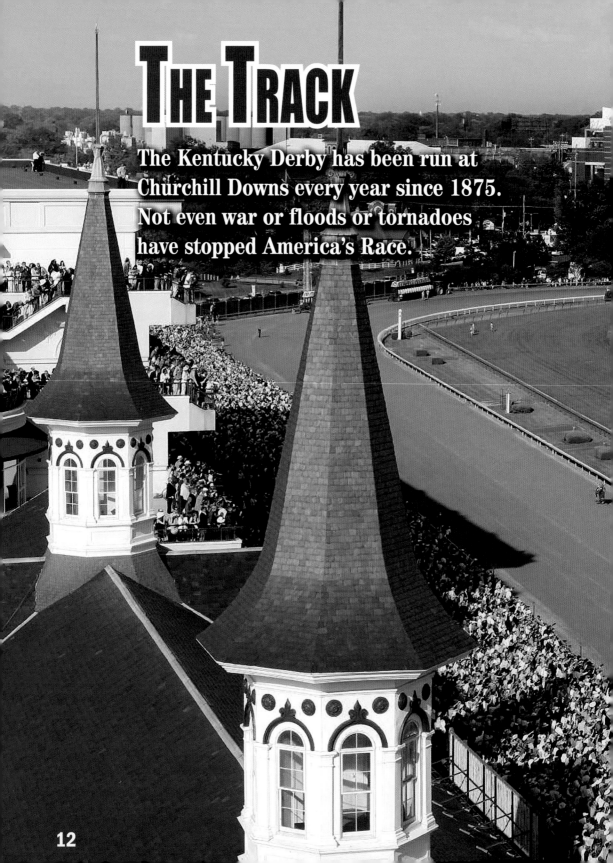

THE TRACK

The Kentucky Derby has been run at Churchill Downs every year since 1875. Not even war or floods or tornadoes have stopped America's Race.

Churchill Downs is most recognized by its twin spires. They were added in 1895. The dirt track is oval-shaped. During the Kentucky Derby, horses run one and one-quarter times around the mile-long (1.6 km) track.

THE RULES

Only three-year-old thoroughbreds may race in the Kentucky Derby. That means that a horse has only one chance to win America's Race. Today, 20 horses compete in the race.

XTREME FACT – The fewest number of horses racing in the Kentucky Derby was three in 1892 and 1905.

Jockey Mike Smith rides Bodemeister during the final stretch of the 2012 Kentucky Derby. After leading the entire race, Bodemeister came in second.

STRATEGY TO WIN

Trainers and jockeys know what makes their horses win. Some horses do well running all out from the starting gate. Others can take the chaos and close quarters in the pack, and still find an opening that puts them out in front. Others gain speed after the last turn. They run in an all-out surge in the final home stretch.

Some Kentucky Derbies are won by a nose and others by several lengths. It's the skill, determination, training, breeding, and even some luck that makes for the most exciting two minutes in sports.

DANGERS

In a sport where 1,000-pound (454-kg) horses blast down a track at speeds of 35 miles per hour (56 kph) carrying 112-pound (51-kg) jockeys, both animals and humans are at great risk. Horses sometimes fall and break their legs. Jockeys are sometimes thrown to the ground. Both riders and horses risk broken bones, paralysis, and sometimes even death.

Eight Belles broke two ankles and had to be put down after taking 2nd place in the 2008 Kentucky Derby. The pain of losing such a great horse was felt by fans everywhere.

19

TRIPLE CROWN

The Kentucky Derby is the first of three races that make up the Triple Crown. The Preakness Stakes is run two weeks later in Baltimore, Maryland. New York's Belmont Stakes is the last race, run three weeks after the Preakness. Only 11 horses have won all 3 of these races:

1919 - Sir Barton

1930 - Gallant Fox

1935 - Omaha

1937 - War Admiral

1941 - Whirlaway

1943 - Count Fleet

1946 - Assault

1948 - Citation

1973 - Secretariat

1977 - Seattle Slew

1978 - Affirmed

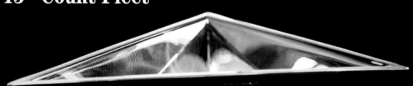

The Triple Crown Trophy was first created in 1950. All 11 winners have since received the trophy.

1978

Affirmed wins the Kentucky Derby.

Affirmed wins at Preakness.

Affirmed wins at Belmont, becoming a Triple Crown winner!

FAMOUS HORSES

Any horse that wins the Kentucky Derby is an amazing thoroughbred. A few horses have run so well they will always be remembered.

First Winner

Aristides won the first Kentucky Derby in 1875. He was 15 hands tall, small for a thoroughbred racehorse. He wasn't supposed to win, just lead the way. But Aristides galloped to victory. A life-sized statue stands at Churchill Downs in his honor.

Winning by the Greatest Distance

Old Rosebud won by eight lengths in 1914.

Johnstown won by eight lengths in 1939.

Whirlaway won by eight lengths in 1941.

Assault won by eight lengths in 1946.

Winning Fillies

Regret won in 1915.

Genuine Risk won in 1980.

Winning Colors won in 1988.

Most Wins

Citation won the Kentucky Derby in 1948. He went on to win a record 19 out of 20 races that same year, including winning the Triple Crown. "He went so fast, he scared me," said Eddie Arcaro, Citation's jockey.

Seattle Slew won every race he was in as a two-year-old and as a three-year-old before winning the 1977 Kentucky Derby. Slew became the only undefeated horse to win the Triple Crown up to that time.

Fastest

Secretariat holds the record for the fastest Kentucky Derby race ever run. "Big Red" won in 1:59.4. Secretariat also holds the fastest track record at the Belmont Stakes for his 1973 run. Secretariat won the Triple Crown that year.

Most Money

Smarty Jones' earnings were $7,613,155 with nine starts, making the 2004 Kentucky Derby winner the highest money earner among Derby winners to date. The next highest was 1987's winner Alysheba, with $6,679,242 in 26 starts.

FAMOUS JOCKEYS

Jockeys are about 5' 4" (1.6 m) tall and weigh an average of 112 pounds (51 kg). Several of these smal but highly skilled, riders have become famous.

First Winner

Youngest Winner

First Hall of Famer

Oliver Lewis, a 19-year-old from Kentucky, rode into history as the winner of the first Kentucky Derby on Aristides on May 17, 1875.

Alonzo Clayton was 15 years old when he won the 1892 Kentucky Derby riding Azra. Today, the minimum age of a Derby jockey is 16.

Isaac Murphy won the 1884, 1890, and 1891 Kentucky Derbies. He was the first jockey elected to the National Museum of Racing and Hall of Fame.

First Woman

Diane Crump was the first woman jockey to ride in the Kentucky Derby. She rode Fathom to a 15th place finish on May 2, 1970. Only six women have ridden in the Derby to date:

- *Diane Crump - 1970*
- *Patricia Cooksey - 1984*
- *Andrea Seefeldt - 1991*
- *Julie Krone - 1992 and 1995*
- *Rosemary Homeister - 2003*
- *Anna Rose Napravnik - 2011*

"Steady Eddie" Arcaro won five Kentucky Derbies in 1938, 1941, 1945, 1948, and 1952. He also won the Triple Crown on Whirlaway in 1941 and in 1948 on Citation. He was known as "The Master."

Bill Hartack won five Kentucky Derbies in only 12 tries. He won in 1957, 1960, 1962, 1964, and 1969. In 1957, Hartack was the first jockey whose horses reached $3 million in earnings. That record held for 10 years.

Oldest Winner

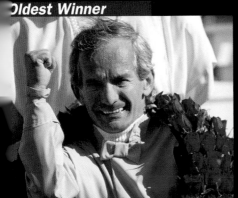

Most Money

Willie "Shoe" Shoemaker won four Kentucky Derbies in 1955, 1959, 1965, and 1986. The 1986 win made him the oldest jockey to win at the age of 54. He competed in 26 Derbies, more than any other jockey.

Pat Day, the 1992 Kentucky Derby winner, has won more prize money than any other Derby-winning jockey to date. Over the course of 8,803 career wins, he has earned just under $298 million.

TRADITIONS

The Kentucky Derby has many unique traditions that have continued year after year.

Fans dress fashionably and wear hats. This is a tradition that came from England's Royal Ascot track.

The traditional Derby-day food is a thick stew called burgoo. The traditional drink is the mint julep.

The song "My Old Kentucky Home" is always sung before the running of the Kentucky Derby.

Jockey Mike Smith sits atop the 2005 Kentucky Derby winner Giacomo. A blanket of roses is traditionally placed over the winning horse. This is why the Kentucky Derby is sometimes called the "Run for the Roses."

THE FINISH

After winning the Kentucky Derby, the horse, jockey, owner, and trainer go to the winner's circle at Churchill Downs to receive their awards. The gold trophy weighs 3.5 pounds (1.6 kg). It is worth about $90,000. Even more exciting is the Derby's "purse," or prize money. The 2012 winner earned nearly $1.5 million, awarded to the horse's owner. It was a great day for a three-year-old horse and its winning team!

Giacomo, the 2005 Kentucky Derby winner, enters the winner's circle.

Jockey Mario Gutierrez (left) and owner J. Paul Reddam (right) celebrate after winning the 138th Kentucky Derby in 2012.

XTREME FACT – Ten percent of the Derby winner's $1.5 million goes to the jockey. That means that for a two-minute race, the jockey earns $1,250 per second!

GLOSSARY

BELMONT STAKES

A race held each year since 1867 for three-year-old thoroughbred horses. Belmont is held in early June at Belmont Park in Elmont, New York. It is the third and final race of the Triple Crown.

BURGOO

A thick stew made of beef, chicken, pork, and vegetables. It is the traditional food eaten at the Kentucky Derby.

FILLY

A female horse.

HAND

A measurement equaling 4 inches (10 cm). Thoroughbreds are usually 15-17 hands tall, measuring from shoulders to ground.

JOCKEY

A person whose job is to ride and race horses. In the Kentucky Derby, a fully-clothed jockey and his or her gear may not weigh more than 126 pounds (57 kg).

LENGTH

In horse racing, the length of one horse from nose to tail. This is approximately 8 feet (2.4 m). The widest margin of victory for any Derby win is eight lengths.

MINT JULEP
An alcoholic drink made of bourbon, crushed ice, sugar, and fresh mint. It is the traditional drink of the Kentucky Derby.

NATIONAL MUSEUM OF RACING AND HALL OF FAME
A museum founded in 1950 in Saratoga Springs, New York. The museum honors American thoroughbred horse racing, and the horses and people who have made it great.

PREAKNESS STAKES
A race held each year since 1873 for three-year-old thoroughbred horses. Preakness is held mid-May at Pimlico Race Course in Baltimore, Maryland. It is the second race leading to the Triple Crown.

PURSE
The overall prize money given to the top finishers in a horse race. The 2012 Kentucky Derby had a $2.2 million purse. The winner received nearly $1.5 million. Second- through fifth-place winners receive smaller amounts.

THOROUGHBRED
A horse breed known for its speed, agility, and spirit.

TRIPLE CROWN
The name for winning three important horse races: Kentucky Derby, Preakness Stakes, and Belmont Stakes. Only 11 horses have won the Triple Crown over 138 years.

INDEX